Fixing Your Finances

Strategies for Long-Term Wealth

Table of Contents

Chapter 1. Introduction

Welcome to "Fixing Your Finances: Strategies for Long-Term Wealth" - the essential Special Report that makes understanding and managing your financial future exciting and empowering! You don't have to be a Wall-Street wizard to secure a prosperous tomorrow. This user-friendly guide is bursting with practical, easy-to-apply strategies designed to help you systematically build long-term wealth. In the pages that follow, we break down complex financial concepts into bite-sized bits of wisdom that promise to transform the way you think about and handle your money. Buy this Special Report today: Your journey towards financial freedom awaits!

Chapter 2. Understanding Personal Finance Basics

Financial well-being often springs from a clear understanding and mastery of personal finance basics. Starting from the ground up allows individuals to make informed decisions about money management, budgeting, investing, and saving, which collectively, build the foundation for a financially secure future.

2.1. The Importance of Personal Finance

Personal finance refers to how individuals manage their money, including their income, expenses, savings, and investments. It is a broad term that encompasses every financial decision an individual or family makes, from planning for future spending to managing debt and retirement savings.

Understanding personal finance is crucial for several reasons. For starters, it gives you control over your income and expenditure. This knowledge equips you to make informed choices about spending, saving, and investing, thereby enabling you to achieve your financial goals. Furthermore, understanding personal finance can also insulate you from financial hardship by helping you build an emergency fund and adequately prepare for retirement.

2.2. Budgeting: Where It All Begins

Budgeting is a critical first step in personal finance. A budget is a plan for your income and expenditures that can help you manage your finances. It involves tracking your monthly income, expenses, and determining the best use of your money based on your financial goals and responsibilities.

Three core elements define a budget:

1. Income: This is the money you earn over a given period.

2. Expenses: These are your costs or expenditures, such as rent, groceries, and electricity.

3. Savings or Deficit: This is what remains when you subtract your expenses from your income.

Creating a budget involves identifying your income and expenses and then adjusting your spending to live within your means while also addressing savings and debt reduction.

2.3. Credit and Debt Management

Credit refers to the ability of an individual to borrow money or access goods or services with the understanding that they will repay the lender at a later date. Credit includes personal loans, mortgages, credit cards, and any other method used to finance a borrower's needs.

Effective debt management is a crucial part of personal finance. Like all tools, credit can be beneficial if used correctly, but it can also lead to debt if mismanaged. By understanding how to manage debt, you can avoid financial pitfalls, maintain a good credit score, and reach your financial goals.

Here are some strategies to effectively manage your debt:

1. Pay off high-interest debt first, referred to as the 'Avalanche Method'.

2. Make more than the minimum payment, which will lessen the time it takes to pay off your debt.

3. Consolidate your debt through a personal loan or balance

transfer credit card to lower interest rates.

2.4. Savings and Investments

Saving involves setting aside a portion of your income for future use. It's money you aim to spend in the future, not today. While saving involves putting money aside for short-term goals, investing is about growing your wealth for long-term goals.

One of the most common forms of savings is an emergency fund, which is a stash of money set aside to cover costs or living expenses in case of emergencies.

Investing involves committing your funds to potentially profitable ventures like stocks, bonds, or real estate with the hope of achieving a return over time. When investing, it's important to create a diversified portfolio to reduce risk.

2.5. Retirement Planning

Retirement planning is about preparing for your future when you will no longer be earning a regular income from employment. In addition to pensions and Social Security, personal savings and investments can greatly contribute to a comfortable retirement.

You should start planning for retirement as early as your first job, even if retirement seems a long way off. The earlier you start, the more money you will accumulate due to the power of compound interest.

2.6. Insurance

Insurance is a financial product designed to reduce financial risks. By paying a regular premium, individuals can protect themselves from financial losses resulting from various risks, like health issues, property damage, accidents, and death.

Having insurance coverage is an integral part of financial wellness as it provides financial protection against unforeseen circumstances.

By understanding these core areas of personal finance, you can set yourself on a path that leads to financial independence and a secure future. But remember, the mastery of personal finance does not occur overnight. It calls for patience, persistence, and a desire to learn and adapt to changing financial circumstances and opportunities.

Chapter 3. Setting Clear and Achievable Financial Goals

Understanding your current financial position and expectations for the future is vital in achieving financial freedom. This chapter will help you establish clear, attainable financial objectives, guide you through the process of drafting your financial plan, and monitor its success.

3.1. Financial Self-Assessment

Before setting goals, take stock of where you are. Understand your assets, liabilities, income streams, expenses, and your overall financial health.

1. Assets: Assets are things that have monetary value, such as your home, car, savings, investments, and retirement funds. Begin by listing all your assets and their estimated value.

2. Liabilities: Liabilities are the debts and financial obligations you owe, including loans and credit card balances.

3. Income streams: Consider how much money you're earning regularly. Include all sources including your salary, royalties, dividends, rental income, and any other income sources.

4. Expenses: Calculate your monthly spending habits. Needs like food, shelter, electricity, and transportation fall under essential expenses while wants like entertainment, eating out, and vacations are non-essential.

Having an overview of your financial condition is the foundation for setting your goals.

3.2. Establishing Clear Financial Goals

Now that you understand your financial situation, let's move on to establishing your targets. Financial goals can be of three types - short-term, medium-term, and long-term objectives.

- Short-term goals (1-3 years): These could include saving for a vacation, paying off small debts, or building an emergency fund.

- Medium-term goals (4-6 years): These might involve saving for a down payment on a house or a car, or funding higher education.

- Long-term goals (>7 years): These are typically retirement savings, paying off a mortgage, or creating a substantial investment portfolio.

When setting goals, follow the SMART method:

- Specific: Your goal should be clear. Instead of saying, "I want to save money," say, "I want to save $10,000 in two years."

- Measurable: You should be able to measure your progress. In the example above, you know you have to save about $416 per month.

- Attainable: Goals should be realistic based on your income and expenses.

- Relevant: Your financial goals should align with your overall life objectives.

- Time-bound: Set a timeline to achieve the goal.

3.3. Creating a Financial Plan

A financial plan acts as a roadmap towards your financial goals. It maps out financial strategies and tactics that will help you meet your objectives. The plan should include budgeting, saving, investing, and managing your debts.

1. Budgeting: A budget is a plan for your money. It maps out your income and expenditures, helping allocate funds for different goals. Make sure to set aside money for both necessities and discretionary spending.

2. Saving: Develop a habit of saving a portion of your income for emergencies, short-term goals, and retirement. Automatically transferring a certain amount to your savings each month can make this effortless.

3. Investing: Enable your money to work for you by investing. Investments can provide additional income streams and boost wealth, providing a roadmap to financial freedom.

4. Debt Management: Plan to pay off existing loans and avoid unnecessary debts. High-interest liabilities, like credit card debt can hamper your financial growth.

3.4. Monitoring and Adjusting Your Financial Plan

A financial plan isn't something you set and forget. You should review it regularly and make adjustments as necessary. Your income could increase, your expenses could change dramatically, or your goals might shift; all of these necessitate adjustments.

Reviewing your plan annually can ensure consistency between your changing situation and financial objectives. Changes in family size, housing, job, or health could necessitate an update to your plan.

A clear and achievable financial goal is the first step towards your financial freedom. Understand your finances, set SMART goals, create a plan to achieve these goals, and continually review and amend your plan as per your changing life situations.

Chapter 4. Budgeting: The Backbone of Financial Freedom

To truly fix your finances and lay the groundwork for long-term wealth, one must start with the crucial step of budgeting. This is a process that, when consistently practiced, can help transform your financial future. In this section, we lay out the necessary tools and techniques to make budgeting both an attainable and lasting habit.

4.1. Understanding the Basics of Budgeting

Since money isn't unlimited, it's essential to know where every cent is going. This is where budgeting comes in, helping you allocate your income towards various categories — necessities, savings, and wants. Proper allocation can prevent overspending, help repay debts, and save for future goals. Here are the primary components of a budget:

- Income: All your sources of income, including your salary, side gigs, dividends, etc.

- Fixed Costs: Regular expenses that don't change significantly over time, such as rent, insurance premiums, etc.

- Variable Costs: Expenses that vary from month to month, such as utilities, groceries, entertainment, etc.

- Goals: Financial aspirations, including short-term goals (like holiday spending) and long-term goals (like retirement).

The process starts by listing your income and expenses, separating costs into fixed and variable categories. Once identified, allocate a portion of your income towards your goals. No goal is too small to start budgeting, the central idea is to make a habit of saving.

4.2. How to Create a Budget

To make a budget, follow these simple steps:

Step 1: Assess your financial situation List every income source, including wages, side gigs, etc., for a clear picture of your monthly inflow.

Step 2: Identify your expenses Track your expenditures over the last three months, separating them into fixed and variable costs. Remember, this includes everything from utility bills to occasional movie nights.

Step 3: Create a financial map After you've earmarked your income and expenses, outline where funds should go. Designate a specific portion of your income for needs, wants, and goals.

Step 4: Implement Your Budget The next step is to keep to the plan you've outlined. A budget is worth it only when you stick by it consistently.

Remember to revisit your budget periodically to make adjustments, especially when faced with significant financial changes.

4.3. Zero-Based Budgeting: A Powerful Technique

Zero-based budgeting (ZBB) is a technique where your income minus your outgo equals zero. The goal is to use every dollar you earn purposefully, balancing the scales between income and expenses. This method might feel restrictive, but it fosters conscious spending, making you cognizant of every dollar spent.

4.4. Practical Tips for Successful Budgeting

While budgeting might seem daunting initially, stacking small, consistent efforts lead to substantial, long-lasting results. Here are some practical tips:

- Start Small: Begin by allocating small amounts towards your savings or goals. As you get comfortable, gradually increase this.

- Track Expenses: Regularly monitor your spending. Several online tools and apps can help with this.

- Be Realistic: Don't create a too-restrictive budget. Cutbacks should not equate to deprivation; ensure there's room for enjoyment too.

- Adapt and Adjust: Life happens, and so do unexpected expenses. Adjust your budget accordingly when required.

- Celebrate Wins: Celebrate milestones to reinforce the positive progress you're making, no matter how small.

4.5. Leveraging Technology for Better Budgeting

Today's tech can be of significant assistance in budgeting. Apps like Mint, YNAB (You Need A Budget), and PocketGuard offer features to track spending, organize expenses, and even give pointers for better budgeting.

4.6. The Envelope System: A Classic Budgeting Approach

The Envelope System is an excellent way for visual learners to budget. Label envelopes for each expense category and put the allocated budget in each one every month. It boils down to simple arithmetic: if you've allocated $100 for dining out and have used up the envelope's contents, no more dining out until next month.

4.7. The 50/30/20 Rule: A Guiding Framework

A quick and easy way to structure your budget is the 50/30/20 rule, wherein:

- 50% of your income goes to necessities (e.g., rent, utilities, groceries).

- 30% of your income is used for lifestyle choices (e.g., dining outs, holidays).

- 20% of your income is saved or invested for your financial goals.

This rule is a starting point, tweak depending on your financial situation and goals.

4.8. Sticking to Your Budget

A critical part of budgeting is maintaining the discipline to stay with it. Make it habit-forming - ensure every dollar is accounted for, and review your progress regularly.

4.9. The Relation Between Budgeting, Debt Payoff, and Wealth Accumulation

A well-managed budget not only helps control spending but also assists in debt payoff and accelerates wealth accumulation. By allocating a specific amount towards debt repayments and savings in your budget, you align your everyday actions with bigger financial goals.

Budgeting is not just about curbing expenses; it's about taking control of your financial future. Implementing these strategies will incentivize you towards building sustainable, long-term wealth - a vital stride towards financial freedom.

Chapter 5. Saving Techniques and Habits for Wealth Accumulation

In the world of personal finance, one essential rule reigns supreme: Money saved is money earned. Yet the path to achievable, sustainable savings isn't always well-defined. Hence, we bring to you the tried-and-tested strategies that will help you to excel at saving and accumulate wealth over time.

5.1. Building a Saving Mindset

The cornerstone of any successful saving strategy begins with cultivating a saving mindset. This isn't something that develops overnight. Instead, it requires deliberate, consistent effort. The first step in fostering this mindset is to change your perception around saving. It is not a burden but a way to secure your financial future. Recognize that saving, no matter how little, will provide you the cushion you need during emergencies, and fund your future endeavors, including retirement, buying a house, or getting an education.

Another element of the saving mindset is understanding the difference between needs and wants. While necessities are essential for survival and should always be covered, wants denote optional desires. By distinguishing between the two, you can effectively reduce unnecessary expenses and redirect those funds to your savings.

Next in line is the habit of tracking your spending. Without a clear idea of where your money goes, it's impossible to identify areas you can cut back on. It will not only expose you to your spending habits but also provide insights into potential overspending.

Lastly, don't overlook patience and discipline. Saving is a methodical long-term process and won't yield immediate results. Keeping this in perspective will help imbue a stronger saving ethos into your financial management.

5.2. Effective Saving Techniques

While the mindset prepares you to save, it's the techniques you employ that shape your saving journey. Below we introduce some fruitful methods you can integrate into your financial plans.

1. **Paying Yourself First**: Prioritize savings by treating it as an essential payment every month, much like rent or a utility bill. Whatever your income may be, aim to set aside a percentage for savings before allocating the rest for expenses. A common rule of thumb is the 50/30/20 rule, directing 50% of your income to needs, 30% to wants, and 20% straight to your savings.

2. **Automating Savings**: If you tend to forget or neglect monthly savings, automation can be a big help. Most banks offer automatic transfers from checking to saving accounts. Scheduling these transfers right after you receive your paycheck ensures that you won't accidentally overspend.

3. **Incremental Increases**: As your income grows, raise your saving contributions correspondingly. An annual increase of even 1% can lead to significant growth over time.

4. **Emergency Fund**: Create an emergency fund to cover any unexpected expenses like a sudden job loss, health crisis, or immediate home repairs. A good starting point is to aim for three to six months' worth of living expenses stashed away in an easily accessible, low-risk account.

5.3. Investment as a Form of Saving

Investing is one of the most effective ways to grow your wealth. It makes your money work for you rather than sitting idly in a bank account. Here are some investment avenues you might consider:

1. **Stocks and Bonds**: Though potentially risky, these can offer substantial returns in the long run. Consider low-cost index funds or ETFs for a diversified portfolio.

2. **401(k) and Individual Retirement Accounts (IRAs)**: These tax-advantaged accounts allow your money to compound over time and provide a substantial nest egg for retirement.

3. **Real Estate**: Rental properties can provide a steady income stream and appreciate over time, providing both immediate and long-term benefits.

4. **Peer-to-Peer Lending**: Though riskier, you can potentially reap higher interest returns by lending to individuals or small businesses via online platforms.

5.4. The Importance of Reviews and Adjustments

Your saving plan is not a "set and forget" approach. It's essential to review and adjust your plan at regular intervals or life changes. A promotion, marriage, relocation, or birth of a child can dramatically change your financial landscape. During these times, revisit your saving and investment strategies to ensure they still align with your altered financial goals and obligations.

In the end, accumulating wealth through savings isn't rocket science, but a continuous process of deliberate habits, wise decisions, and regular adjustments. By adopting a long-term, future-oriented perspective, you can turn the act of saving from being a daily struggle to becoming an empowering journey towards financial independence. Embrace these saving techniques and habits, and let the amazing power of compound interest fuel your wealth growth for decades to come.

Chapter 6. Investment Basics: Taking Your Savings to the Next Level

The world of investments can be daunting especially when you're just starting out. But worry not, this part of our special report aims to demystify the complexities and give you the tools to take those hard-earned savings and grow them into a bountiful financial harvest.

6.1. The Power of Investment

Investing is not simply about hoarding money but about putting it to work. Instead of letting your savings sit in a bank account, investing lets your money grow. It exposes your savings to the potential of higher returns over the long term, especially when compared to traditional savings accounts or fixed deposits that give minimal interest.

The core idea behind investing is the concept of compound interest, termed the "eighth wonder of the world" by none other than Albert Einstein. Simply put, compound interest is "interest on interest". It's the process where the interest, in addition to the principal, earns interest. Over time, your wealth does not just increase but snowballs!

6.2. Types of Investments

When we talk about investments, it's not a one-size-fits-all scenario. There are a variety of investment vehicles and each comes with a different risk-return profile.

1. **Stocks:** These are shares of a company. By purchasing them, you own a tiny fraction of the company and get to participate in its

growth - and risks.

2. **Bonds:** These are essentially loans you give to a company or a government. In return, you receive a periodic interest payment and the initial amount (principal) on maturity.

3. **Mutual funds:** Investment funds that pool money from multiple investors to invest in a diversified portfolio of stocks, bonds and other assets.

4. **ETFs (Exchange Traded Funds):** These are similar to mutual funds but trade like stocks on an exchange.

5. **Real Estate:** This includes investing in housing, commercial properties, rental properties, etc.

6. **Commodities:** Investing in physical goods like gold, oil, etc.

Selection of the right type of investment depends on your financial goals, risk tolerance, and investment horizon.

6.3. Setting Investment Goals

Keeping sight of your financial goals is key to building wealth. Are you saving for retirement? A down payment on a house? Your child's college fees? Depending on these purposes, your investment approach will vary.

6.4. Risk and Return

Every investment vehicle comes with a different degree of risk and potential returns. Generally, higher-risk investments offer higher potential returns, while low-risk ones offer relatively lower returns.

Charting your risk tolerance - a combination of your financial capacity to absorb losses and your emotional comfort with volatility - is an essential part of your investment journey.

6.5. Importance of Diversification

"Diversify, diversify, diversify!" It's not just a catchy phrase but one of the fundamental principles of investing. The saying, "Don't put all your eggs in one basket," fittingly explains the concept.

Diversification involves spreading your investments across different asset classes - stocks, bonds, real estate, commodities, etc. It reduces your overall risk by ensuring that potential losses from a single investment are offset by gains in others.

6.6. Building an Investment Portfolio

Start by assessing your financial goals, risk tolerance, and time horizon. Once defined, match these with the appropriate asset allocation - the percent split among different asset classes.

Discipline and consistency are key to an investment journey's success. Regularly investing a fixed amount, rather than sporadic large amounts, is advisable. This method, known as 'Dollar Cost Averaging,' reduces the impact of short-term market volatility on your investments.

6.7. Conclusion

Investing may feel like navigating a labyrinth at first, but once you get the hang of it, it becomes exciting. With the concepts we've covered, you're equipped to enter this complex world with confidence. Dip your toes in the water and get started; your future self is guaranteed to thank you!

Next, we will discuss particular investment options in more detail and show you how to manage and track your investments. Stay tuned for an exciting financial journey ahead!

Chapter 7. Managing Debt and Building Credit Score

In comprehending our financial health, two aspects play an integral role - debt management and credit score building. To navigate the world of credit and debts successfully, understanding these levers is essential.

7.1. Debt Management

Managing one's debts effectively is the cornerstone to achieving a strong financial standing. Unmanaged debts can derail our financial plans and lead to unnecessary stress. To secure a better financial future, adopting a strategic approach to your debts is imperative.

7.2. Understanding Different Types of Debts

Differentiating between good and bad debts is the first step in this journey. Traditionally, 'good debt' is viewed as an investment that will generate long-term income or increase in value. For instance, student loans are considered good debt as they are an investment in one's future earning potential. On the other hand, consumer debts, primarily credit cards, are often labeled as 'bad debt' because they can accrue high interest and do not contribute to your long-term financial growth.

It's crucial to understand the nature of your debts and prioritize repayment accordingly. Typically, one should seek to first clear the high-interest 'bad debts'.

7.3. Debt Repayment Strategies

Two major debt repayment strategies frequently employed are the Avalanche and Snowball methods.

The 'Debt Avalanche' method prioritizes paying down debt with the highest interest rates. Once the highest-interest debt is paid off, move to the next one in line.

In contrast, the 'Debt Snowball' method advocates for focusing on the smallest debt first, regardless of interest. Once you've paid off the smallest debt, you proceed to the next smallest, eventually ending up with larger loans.

The 'Avalanche' method is mathematically sound since it minimizes the amount of interest you'll pay, but the 'Snowball' method can be more psychologically satisfying, providing quick victories that can motivate you to keep going.

7.4. Creating a Debt Repayment Plan

The first step in creating your repayment plan is to organize your debts. List out all of your loans, interest rates, and the minimum payments. Decide which repayment strategy, Snowball or Avalanche, suits your needs best, and start scheduling your monthly payments accordingly. Remember to focus on one project at a time while not neglecting to make minimum payments on your other debts.

7.5. Building Your Credit Score

Having a solid credit score is the bedrock for financial management. Your credit score can affect numerous aspects of your life, from qualifying for loans or mortgages to renting an apartment or even job opportunities in some fields.

7.6. Understanding Your Credit Score

Your credit score is a three-digit number derived from detailed information about your credit history. It represents your creditworthiness or, in simpler terms, your capacity and likeliness to repay borrowed money.

Your credit score is used by lenders, landlords, and employers to gauge the risk they are taking on by doing business with you. It is generated based on your credit report, which includes previous and existing loans, repayment history, and total outstanding debts.

There are several credit scoring models, but FICO Score is the most widely used, with scores ranging from 300 (poor credit) to 850 (exceptional credit).

7.7. Ways to Improve Your Credit Score

Building a robust credit score doesn't happen overnight but with proper measures, it can gradually improve.

1. Pay Your Bills on Time: The most effective way to improve your credit score is to pay all your bills and loans on time. Your payment history carries a substantial weight in your credit score calculation.

2. Keep Your Credit Utilization Low: Credit utilization is the percentage of your total available credit that you're currently using. A lower credit utilization ratio suggests that you're not overly reliant on credit and poses less risk to lenders.

3. Maintain Old Credit Accounts: The length of your credit history has a positive impact on your credit score. Therefore, it can be

beneficial to keep older credit accounts open, even if you don't use them regularly.

4. Diversify Your Credit Mix: Having a mix of credit types - for instance, credit cards, mortgage, auto loan - can have a positive impact on your credit score. It shows that you can manage a range of credit products.

Remember, the journey to financial health is a marathon, not a sprint. By managing debt effectively and gradually building up your credit score, you can lay a solid foundation for future financial success.

Chapter 8. Risk Management: Essential Insurance Knowledge

Understanding risk management is crucial to safeguarding your financial future. In this section, we delve deep into the world of insurance. From homeowner's insurance to life insurance, you'll learn why policies matter, how they can serve as a financial safety net, and keys to navigating the vast marketplace of coverages.

8.1. Understanding Insurance: Why It's Important

The concept of insurance is built on a simple idea: pooling of risk. People pay into an insurance pool, managed by an insurance company, and in the event of misfortune (like an accident, health issue, or property damage), the insured person can make a claim. The insurer pays out from this pool, effectively dissipating an individual's risk across the pool of insured people. Insurance is about managing risk effectively to protect individuals from financial losses.

8.2. Types of Insurance: Knowing Your Options

There are many types of insurance policies available, each designed to protect against different kinds of risks.

- **Life Insurance** isn't for you – it's for those you leave behind. If you have dependents who rely on your income, life insurance can replace that income should anything happen to you.

- **Health Insurance** is designed to cover the cost of medical care. It is essential to protect against financial disasters caused by major illness or injury.

- **Homeowner's Insurance** protects against damage to your home and possessions. It also provides liability coverage should someone be injured while on your property.

- **Car Insurance** is legally required for all drivers and covers the cost of damage to your vehicle and other vehicles in the event of an accident.

- **Disability Insurance** replaces a portion of your income if you are unable to work due to illness or injury.

- **Long-Term Care Insurance** is designed to cover the cost of personal and custodial care for people with chronic illnesses, disabilities, or other conditions.

Knowing your options is a good initial step. But the real challenge begins when you need to choose and manage your insurance policies wisely.

8.3. Choosing the Right Insurance: A Decision Guide

The key to wise insurance decisions is to evaluate your needs based on your lifestyle, dependents, health, assets, risk factors, and financial goals. It involves asking yourself a series of questions:

- What types of risks am I exposed to?

- What financial impact could these risks have if they were to happen?

- Is the cost of insuring against these risks affordable and does it make financial sense?

Once you've assessed your risks, it's time to comparison shop. Look at different insurers, their policy offerings, premiums, coverage limits, and exclusions. Remember, the cheapest policy isn't necessarily the best. Look for value – a balance between the coverage you want and the premiums you can comfortably afford.

8.4. Managing Your Insurance: Essential Policies for Your Financial Plan

Effective risk management involves reassessing your insurance needs at different life stages and adjusting your coverage accordingly. Here's a recommended insurance strategy for different stages:

- **Young Adults:** This group generally benefits from health insurance (often through an employer), renters insurance if renting, car insurance, and potentially life insurance if they have dependents.

- **Families:** Add in life insurance to replace lost income should a breadwinner pass away and disability insurance to replace income if work is suspended because of health. Homeowner's insurance becomes necessary when buying a house.

- **Older Adults:** Long-term care insurance becomes more important in the later stages of life, especially if you have a family history of chronic ailments.

8.5. When Insurance Isn't Enough: Other Risk Management Strategies

Insurance isn't the only way to manage risk. Other financial tools and strategies can complement your insurance coverage and provide additional protection. These could include creating an emergency fund, diversifying your investments, structuring your business to protect personal assets, and incorporating legal contracts to manage business-related risks.

8.6. Conclusion: Harnessing Insurance as a Power Tool

Insurance isn't a static element of your financial plan—it should adapt as your life and needs change. Harness the power of insurance by viewing it as a dynamic tool to manage life's unpredictable risks. Make it a practice to review your coverage annually, and don't hesitate to adjust your policies as your circumstances evolve.

Remember, understanding and managing insurance is a cornerstone in the foundation of your financial independence. When done correctly – it's like a financial safety net, poised to catch you, your family, and your assets when life's curveballs come your way.

Chapter 9. Retirement Planning for a Secure Future

Retirement planning is an essential aspect of achieving long-term financial stability. However, many people consider the task formidable, primarily because of the vast array of investment instruments, fluctuating market scenarios, and complicated legislations. This section aims to demystify these complexities and empower you with a simple step-by-step approach to planning your secure retirement.

9.1. Determining Your Retirement Needs

The first, and most crucial, step towards retirement planning is determining your retirement needs. Start by estimating the annual income you'll need to maintain your current lifestyle. A common rule of thumb is to aim for an income equivalent to 70-80% of your pre-retirement salary. However, your specific requirements may vary based on your current spending and saving habits, desired lifestyle post retirement, and life expectancy.

9.2. Creating a Savings Plan

Once you get an insight into your retirement needs, it's time to create a savings plan to meet those needs. If you save too little, you risk running out of money during retirement. If you save too much, you may unnecessarily deprive yourself of present comforts. To avoid both extremes, you need a well-drafted savings plan. This involves setting clear financial goals, designating a specific amount for saving every month, and regularly monitoring and adjusting your savings behavior based on evolving financial circumstances.

9.3. Building an Investment Portfolio

Investing is not just about saving money, but also making it grow. A well-structured investment portfolio not only accumulate wealth over the years, but also generates passive income during your retirement years, minimizing the risk of running out of money. While devising your investment strategy, consider a mix of different investment options to diversify risk. These may include retirement accounts like 401(k) or Individual Retirement Accounts (IRAs), stocks, bonds, mutual funds, real estate, etc. Also, be mindful of the shares of each type of investment in your portfolio. Typically, riskier assets like stocks should constitute a lower percentage, and safer assets like bonds, a higher percentage.

9.4. Optimizing Tax Benefits

Numerous tax-advantaged retirement accounts are available that not only offer deductions for your contributions but also allow your savings to grow tax-deferred. These include Traditional IRA, Roth IRA, 401(k) plans, and others. Properly leveraging these accounts can significantly augment your retirement corpus.

9.5. Planning for Health Care

Many people underestimate the potential medical expenses in their retirement years. Health care costs have historically risen faster than the general inflation rate, and this trend is likely to continue. Therefore, it's essential to factor in the cost of healthcare, including that of long-term care, if required, in your retirement planning. Consider Health Savings Accounts (HSAs) and Long-Term Care Insurance for this purpose.

9.6. Estate Planning

Estate planning, though often overlooked, is a key element of retirement planning. Having a proper estate plan—essentially a will or trust—ensures that your wealth is distributed as per your wishes after your death. A well-structured estate plan can also offer significant tax advantages.

9.7. Reviewing the Plan

Just as you routinely monitor your health, it is prudent to review your retirement plan regularly—preferably annually, or whenever a significant financial or life event occurs. This way, you can ensure that your plan remains aligned with your current financial situation, long-term goals, and market conditions.

By incorporating these strategies in your retirement planning, you'll be well on your way to a secure, worry-free post-retirement life. Remember that retirement planning is a journey, not a destination. It requires discipline, consistency, and flexibility to adapt to changing circumstances. As daunting as it might sound, with an effective plan in place, you're already ahead of most people. Start today, if you haven't already, and secure your future!

Chapter 10. Tax Planning: A Crucial Ingredient for Wealth Creation

It's often noted that 'nothing is certain but death and taxes'. While mortality may remain beyond our control, we can still have a say over how much we pay in taxes each year. Tax planning is an essential element of a strategic approach to wealth management. It involves understanding your current position, your financial goals, and how the tax laws can influence both these elements to maximize your returns and minimize your tax liability.

10.1. Understanding Your Tax Brackets

Tax brackets determine the rate at which your income is taxed. Each country has tax laws that categorize income levels into tax brackets. In the United States, for instance, tax brackets are a range of incomes taxed at a given rate. Tax rates often increase as income increases, a system known as progressive taxation.

Understanding your tax bracket is crucial to effective tax planning. This knowledge enables you to make informed financial decisions, such as when to sell an asset, buy a property, or cash out on investments.

10.2. Utilizing Tax Deductions and Credits

The law provides several opportunities to lower your tax bill through deductions and credits. A tax deduction decreases your taxable income, while a tax credit reduces the amount of tax owed.

For example, you can deduct certain expenses such as home mortgage interest, educational expenses, medical and dental expenses, or charitable donations from your taxable income. Each dollar you deduct from your income translates into a tax saving equal to your marginal tax rate.

Tax credits, although fewer than deductions, offer dollar-for-dollar reductions in your tax bill. They include education credits, retirement savings contributions credits, child and dependent care credits, and more.

10.3. The Role of Retirement Planning

Apart from securing your financial future, retirement accounts like 401(k)s and Individual Retirement Accounts (IRAs) can offer significant tax advantages. Contributions to traditional 401(k) or IRA can be made pre-tax, reducing your taxable income for the year.

These funds grow tax-deferred until withdrawal, allowing your investment returns to compound over time. On withdrawal, however, you will owe income taxes on the amount.

Roth 401(k)s or IRAs, on the other hand, are funded with after-tax dollars; but both contributions and earnings can be withdrawn tax-free at retirement, subject to certain conditions.

10.4. Investment and Capital Gains Tax

Investments are a backbone of wealth creation, and their related tax implications are a critical aspect of long-term financial planning.

Essentially, the profits you earn from selling an investment are known as capital gains, taxed under short-term or long-term capital gains tax rates.

Short-term capital gain taxes apply to investments held for less than a year and are usually taxed at ordinary income tax rates. On the other hand, long-term capital gains tax rates apply to investments held for more than a year and are generally lower.

Planning when to buy and sell your investments can help you take advantage of these differing tax rates.

10.5. Estate Planning

Estate planning involves determining how your assets will be distributed upon your death in the most efficient manner possible. It aims to ensure the maximum amount of wealth is passed on to your chosen beneficiaries while minimizing estate taxes.

Advanced estate planning strategies can provide significant tax savings. For example, you could use trusts to distribute assets, which can bypass probate and provide tax benefits.

With the complexities surrounding the tax system, professional financial guidance will likely prove beneficial. Tax planning isn't a one-off event but instead, a continuous process that helps align your tax-saving strategies with your wealth-creation goals.

By grasping these paradigms of tax planning, you position yourself toward a wealthier and more secure financial future. After all, it's not just what you make—it's also what you get to keep that matters.

Remember: To stay ahead of the tax game, awareness of the law, vigilance in record-keeping, and understanding of investment and savings options are paramount. Make the tax system work for you, not against you!

Chapter 11. Establishing and Preserving Your Financial Legacy

Building a robust financial legacy requires strategic and ongoing planning. It's much more than simply amassing wealth—it involves establishing clear objectives, aligning your financial practices with your goals, and creating a system of preservation that ensures your legacy endures for future generations. Let's delve into strategies for establishing and safeguarding your financial legacy.

11.1. Understanding Your Financial Legacy

Safeguarding your financial legacy begins with understanding what it entails. At its core, your financial legacy comprises the resources you'll leave behind for your successors. It encompasses your savings, investments, physical assets, liability management, and, importantly, your intentions for distributing your wealth. The clearer you are about your financial legacy's composition, the better positioned you will be to manage and grow it.

Thinking long-term, it's crucial to align your financial legacy with your values. Do you wish to fund your children's education? Perhaps you'd like to contribute to your favorite charity? By defining these intents early, you can channel your efforts effectively.

11.2. Setting Clear Financial Objectives

First, identify clear financial objectives. Your financial objectives constitute the stepping stones towards achieving your desired financial legacy. These could be short-term (like buying a home in the next five years), mid-term (such as paying for college for your children), or long-term (planning for a comfortable retirement).

With well-defined targets, you can create strategies optimized to achieve these objectives.

Remember to make these them:

- Specific: Clearly state what you want to achieve.

- Measurable: Attach specific numbers to your goals.

- Achievable: Ensure your objective is realistic.

- Relevant: Align your goal with your broader financial strategy.

- Time-bound: Allocate a specific timeline to achieve your target.

By setting S.M.A.R.T. objectives, you are laying a solid foundation for a strong and enduring financial legacy.

11.3. Choosing the Right Investment Strategy

To amass wealth that outlives you, choosing the right investment strategy is pivotal. This involves understanding your risk appetite, diversifying your investments, and allocating funds across different asset classes.

Investing for your legacy is a long-game strategy. Usually, lower-risk investments (like bonds or CDs) do not yield as much as higher-risk investment options (like stocks), but they provide greater stability over the short term. For a durable financial legacy, incorporating a mix of low- and high-risk assets can provide optimal balance.

Diversification is crucial for managing risk. By investing in various asset classes (e.g., stocks, bonds, real estate, etc.), you reduce the risk of damaging losses. Spreading your investments minimizes the impact of any one sector's poor performance on your overall investment portfolio.

11.4. On Liability and Debt Management

While accruing wealth is significant in building a financial legacy, managing liabilities and debts is equally vital. Poor debt management can sap away at the wealth you're striving to create. Thus, it's essential to have strategies in place for handling existing debts and avoiding unnecessary future liabilities.

One way to tackle existing debts is to create a payment plan that prioritizes debts with the highest interest rates. By focusing on these 'expensive' debts first, you can minimize the interest accrued over time.

Be mindful about incurring future debts; ask yourself if the debt you're about to assume is beneficial or detrimental in the long run. Mortgages or student loans, for example, might be considered 'good' debts because they are investments in assets that could appreciate over time or yield higher income.

11.5. Estate Planning Essentials

A crucial aspect of preserving your financial legacy is proactive estate planning. Estate planning involves organizing your assets and determining how they will be distributed upon your demise. It's about making your intentions concerning your wealth clear, reducing potential disputes and uncertainties for your heirs.

Your estate plan should include key legal instruments such as:

- A will: This legal document details who will receive your assets and when.

- A trust: This allows you to transfer assets to a trustee, who manages them for your beneficiaries.

- Power of attorney: This grants someone you trust the authority to make financial decisions on your behalf if you're unable to.

- Health care directive: This specifies what medical actions should be taken if you're unable to make decisions for yourself.

Estate planning is often overlooked, but managing it early can minimize estate taxes and ensure your wealth benefits those you care for in the ways you intend.

11.6. Engaging Financial Professionals

Maintaining a growing and lasting financial legacy often involves complexity and requires specialized knowledge. It can be beneficial to engage financial professionals such as financial advisors, accountants, and lawyers for expert guidance. They help you maximize your wealth, stay updated with legal changes, navigate tax implications, and ensure your legacy strategies are on track.

However, when hiring professionals, it's wise to research their reputation, qualifications, and fee structures. Transparent communication about your legacy objectives is paramount for fruitful collaboration.

In conclusion, creating and preserving a financial legacy is a journey—one that requires clear objectives, smart investments, robust liability management, proactive estate planning, and often, partnering with financial professionals. It's not merely about leaving wealth behind; it's about leaving a legacy that echoes your values and meets your objectives for generations to come. Act today and secure your family's future.